Journey to Freedom®

BROWN v. BOARD OF EDUCATION

BY BARBARA A. SOMERVILL

"WE CONCLUDE THAT IN THE FIELD OF
PUBLIC EDUCATION, THE DOCTRINE OF
'SEPARATE BUT EQUAL' HAS NO PLACE."

CHIEF JUSTICE EARL WARREN,
BROWN v. BOARD OF EDUCATION,
MAY 17, 1954

The Child's World

Cover and page 4 caption: A mother and daughter sat in front of the U.S. Supreme Court building in 1954. The newspaper in the mother's hand announced the Court's school integration ruling.

Content Consultant: Cheryl Brown Henderson, president and CEO, Brown Foundation for Educational Equity, Excellence and Research

Published in the United States of America by The Child's World®
1980 Lookout Drive, Mankato, MN 56003-1705
800-599-READ • www.childsworld.com

ACKNOWLEDGEMENTS

The Child's World®: Mary Berendes, Publishing Director

The Design Lab: Kathleen Petelinsek, Design; Gregory Lindholm, Page Production

Red Line Editorial: Holly Saari, Editorial Direction

PHOTOS

Cover and page 4: Bettmann/Corbis

Interior: Bettmann/Corbis, 5, 9; AP Images, 7, 8, 13, 17, 18, 22, 24, 26; Eudora Welty/Corbis, 11; Lewis Wickes Hine/Library of Congress, 12; Rudolph Faircloth/AP Images, 14; Warren K. Leffler/Library of Congress, 15; Brown Family Collection, 16; Thomas J. O'Halloran/Library of Congress, 21, 27; John T. Bledsoe/Library of Congress, 23

LIBRARY OF CONGRESS CATALOGING-IN-PUBLICATION DATA

Somervill, Barbara A.
 Brown v. Board of Education / by Barbara A. Somervill.
   p. cm. — (Journey to freedom)
 Includes bibliographical references and index.
 ISBN 978-1-60253-119-2 (library bound : alk. paper)
 1. Segregation in education—Law and legislation—United States—Juvenile literature. 2. Discrimination in education—Law and legislation—United States—Juvenile literature. [1. African Americans—Civil rights—Juvenile literature.] I. Title. II. Title: Brown versus Board of Education. III. Series.
 KF4155.Z9S628 2009
 344.73'0798—dc22

                          2009003641

CONTENTS

Chapter One

FIGHTING INEQUALITY, 5

Chapter Two

SEPARATE, BUT NOT EQUAL, 8

Chapter Three

FIVE CASES IN ONE, 13

Chapter Four

A HISTORIC DECISION, 17

Chapter Five

BROWN V. BOARD'S IMPACT, 23

Time Line, 28

Glossary, 30

Further Information, 31

Index, 32

George McLaurin was separated from his classmates at the University of Oklahoma in 1948.

Chapter One

FIGHTING INEQUALITY

In 1938, the U.S. Supreme Court ruled that states providing **graduate school** programs for whites had to offer "separate but equal" programs for blacks. The "separate but equal" **doctrine** said that black and white people could be taught in separate schools only if the schools were equal.

George McLaurin, a black American, was accepted at the University of Oklahoma's graduate school of education in 1948. Because of the "separate but equal" doctrine, he attended class by himself or sat at a desk roped off from other students. He ate in a separate section of the cafeteria. He studied in a separate part of the library. McLaurin decided to sue the University of Oklahoma to challenge this policy.

The United States court system is made up of several levels of courts. The highest and most important court is the U.S. Supreme Court. If someone disagrees with a lower court's ruling, that person can file an **appeal** *in hopes that a higher court will change the ruling. The Supreme Court is the highest court to which a person can appeal a ruling. The Supreme Court's decision cannot be appealed. Also, once the Supreme Court rules on an issue, lower courts must follow the ruling in similar cases.*

Thurgood Marshall became McLaurin's lawyer. Marshall was a lawyer for the National Association for the Advancement of Colored People (NAACP). This group was set up to work for **constitutional** rights for blacks. The NAACP was working to end unequal education for black students. The group decided that fighting inequality at a college would be a good place to start.

Marshall argued in court that McLaurin was not getting an equal education at the university. In 1950, the Supreme Court ruled in McLaurin's favor. The University of Oklahoma was forced to end its **segregation** policies.

McLaurin's **lawsuit** was successful, but many similar ones around this time were not. In 1947, a black farmer named Levi Pearson from South Carolina sued his local school board to get a school bus for his children. He claimed that since the district provided buses for whites, it should do the same for blacks. Local whites blocked Pearson's efforts. He lost credit at stores and local banks. He could not buy farm supplies or sell his crops.

The NAACP's strategy of fighting for equal but still segregated schools was not the answer. The NAACP and its lawyers decided to file lawsuits. They hoped the rulings in these lawsuits would lead to school **integration**. This would allow black and white children to be educated in the same classrooms. The NAACP's goal was to have the Supreme Court overturn the "separate but equal" ruling that was decided in *Plessy v. Ferguson* in 1896.

On May 17, 1954, Chief Justice Earl Warren read the Supreme Court's ruling in the *Brown v. Board of Education* case. The words he delivered would become historic and life-altering for all children. He said, "We conclude that in the field of public education the doctrine of 'separate but equal' has no place. Separate facilities are inherently unequal."

Brown v. Board of Education was a milestone in the fight to ensure equal opportunity for all people, regardless of race or ethnicity. The *Brown* case proved that segregated schools were unequal. From that point on, children of all races were allowed to learn together in the same schools.

*The NAACP was founded in 1909. It has served an important role in helping blacks and other **minority groups** gain full constitutional rights.*

Black and white boys attending the same school in Washington DC in 1954

The U.S. Constitution gained the Fourteenth Amendment in 1868.

Chapter Two

SEPARATE, BUT NOT EQUAL

he end of the U.S. Civil War in 1865 should have provided great opportunities for black people. In 1868, blacks were granted full citizenship under the Fourteenth **Amendment** to the U.S. **Constitution**. The amendment included equal protection under the law for black citizens. But the reality for blacks was quite different, especially in the South where slavery's **aftermath** was most present. Many people did not want blacks to be equal under the law.

By the 1870s, state governments in the South passed many laws to limit the rights of blacks. These were called Jim Crow laws. The laws made racial segregation a way of life.

In the late 1800s, a Louisiana Jim Crow law required separate train facilities for blacks. They were forced to ride in railroad cars labeled "colored." The cars had hard wooden seats and little fresh air. The "colored" cars often rode directly behind the coal cars, so black travelers had to breathe in coal dust. In 1892, a black man named Homer Plessy was put in jail for sitting in the whites-only car of the East Louisiana Railroad. He filed a lawsuit to challenge this Jim Crow law.

The court case became known as *Plessy v. Ferguson*. Plessy's lawyer claimed that separate railroad cars and train station waiting rooms violated the Fourteenth Amendment. The case was unsuccessful in the U.S. District Court of Louisiana. In 1896, *Plessy v. Ferguson* went to the U.S. Supreme Court. The Court ruled that if the facilities were separate but equal, no rights were violated. The ruling set in place what became known as the "separate but equal" doctrine. It also ended the chance for blacks to receive equal protection under the law—or equal treatment by whites.

Signs directed this man to the blacks-only waiting room at a train station.

The *Plessy* court decision was used to further segregate and **discriminate**. Blacks throughout the South were forced to use separate water fountains, restrooms, and restaurants. They were made to sit in the backs of buses. They were also separated in movie theaters, stores, and schools. Southern, white lawmakers said such actions were legal because everything was separate but equal.

But there was little equality in these separate places. In the mid-1900s, white children in Clarendon County, South Carolina, attended school for nine months of the year. Class sizes were small. School was held in buildings with heat, water, and restrooms. Students sat at comfortable desks. They studied from new textbooks.

For black children, the school term did not last longer than six months. No school was held during planting and harvesting seasons because many black children had to work in the fields during those months. Class sizes were large. Sometimes only a few teachers taught all the school's grade levels. Black schools were little more than broken-down cabins. Often they had no running water. Students used outhouses instead of indoor toilets. School buildings had no heat in the winter, and the roofs leaked. Students sat at rickety tables. They used out-of-date textbooks.

Despite these differences, Clarendon County officials still said that all schools were equal. The county's board of education spent $179 a year on

A man using the colored entrance to a theater in the mid-1930s

each white student and $43 a year on each black student. This type of difference existed in many parts of the country. Public schools in Atlanta, Georgia, spent $570 on each white student per year and only $228 on each black student.

Segregated schools created a cycle of **poverty**. Without a good education, most blacks could only find jobs as maids, laborers, and farm workers. Many black parents wanted to change the schools. They wanted better lives for their children. Parents understood that a good education could improve their children's lives.

The NAACP knew black children were being denied access to the best education. The group also knew that education was important for children to succeed in life. The NAACP decided to fight this inequality. In the 1930s and 1940s, the NAACP's lead lawyer, Charles Houston, and several other lawyers, including Thurgood Marshall, worked on cases to end school segregation.

In the 1940s, black students of different grade levels were often taught in the same classroom.

Chapter Three

FIVE CASES IN ONE

I n 1948, the NAACP decided to challenge the "separate but equal" doctrine of the *Plessy* case. The NAACP was fighting more than inequality. They were fighting the difficult issue of segregation. Lawyers and members of the NAACP planned a strategy. It was clear that black parents needed help getting equal education for their children. In the early 1950s, the NAACP helped parents file lawsuits against local school boards.

Five court cases challenging school segregation were filed in different parts of the country. The cases were:

- *Briggs v. Elliot* in South Carolina
- *Davis v. County School Board of Prince Edward County* in Virginia

- *Belton (Bulah) v. Gebhart* in Delaware
- *Brown v. Board of Education of Topeka* in Kansas
- *Bolling v. Sharpe* in Washington DC

The *Briggs v. Elliot* case represented black parents in Clarendon County, South Carolina, who wanted school buses and access to better schools for their children. The case was named for Harry Briggs, who was one of the **plaintiffs**. The federal district court ruled that the county had to make black and white schools equal, but it did not rule to end school segregation. The court ruling was appealed.

Davis v. County School Board of Prince Edward County represented 117 black students from Virginia's R. R. Moton High School. The all-black school was run-down and overcrowded. Some students attended classes in shacks. The students went on a strike led by one of their 16-year-old classmates, Barbara Rose Johns. She wrote to the NAACP asking for help. The NAACP filed a lawsuit for the students, but the court ruled in favor of the school board. The court ruling was appealed.

A segregated classroom in South Carolina in the early 1950s

In *Belton (Bulah) v. Gebhart,* an NAACP lawyer filed a lawsuit for Ethel Belton and Sarah Bulah. They were two parents of black students. In the *Belton* case, black high school students had to travel an hour away from their homes to attend a segregated school. In the *Bulah* case, no school bus was provided for black elementary children. The judge ruled that the black children must be allowed to attend the white schools, but did not overturn the "separate but equal" doctrine. The court ruling was appealed.

A group of people marching for integrated schools and other equal rights in the early 1960s

15

In *Brown v. Board of Education of Topeka,* the NAACP filed a lawsuit on behalf of 13 black parents and their children. It challenged a Kansas law that allowed segregated elementary schools. In 1950, the NAACP asked black parents to try to enroll their children in nearby white schools. The parents were not allowed to do so. School officials and lawyers said segregated schools were equal in Topeka. The NAACP had to challenge the "separate but equal" doctrine. This case was named after one of the plaintiffs, Oliver Brown. The federal district court ruled in favor of the school board. The court ruling was appealed.

In *Bolling v. Sharpe,* the NAACP represented more than ten black students in a case against a Washington DC high school. The students attended an overcrowded black school and tried to enroll in a new white school where some of the classrooms were empty. Their case was named for one of the plaintiffs, Spottswood Bolling Jr. The federal district court ruled against the plaintiffs. The court ruling was appealed.

These five cases were appealed to the Supreme Court. When the cases reached the Court, they were combined under the heading of the Kansas case, *Brown v. Board of Education.*

Oliver Brown, for whom the *Brown v. Board of Education* case was named

The nine Supreme Court justices who ruled on *Brown v. Board of Education*

Chapter Four

A HISTORIC DECISION

rown v. Board of Education reached the Supreme Court's **docket** in 1951. The Court first heard the case in 1952. But, because the justices had very different opinions on the case, Chief Justice Fred Vinson postponed the Court's decision. During this time, scholars worked to gather information that would show how the ruling in the *Plessy* case went against the Fourteenth Amendment. Chief Justice Vinson died during this period. Earl Warren was appointed to become the new chief justice. In December of 1953, the Court heard the *Brown* case again.

NAACP lawyer Thurgood Marshall led the plaintiffs' legal team. Marshall stood before the nine Supreme Court justices and gave his argument. Although he had no microphone, his voice boomed throughout the courtroom.

Marshall said that segregation in schools needed to end. He argued that money and schools were not the worst problems with "separate but equal" education. He stated that black children suffered because segregation existed. NAACP lawyers presented information about

Thurgood Marshall was a powerful speaker in the courtroom.

the damaging emotional effect segregated schools had on black children. Dr. Kenneth Clark, a professor at City College of New York, had studied this negative effect. The results of his study proved there was emotional harm done to children by segregating them by race.

On May 17, 1954, nearly a year and a half after the Court first heard the case, it ruled on *Brown v. Board of Education*. Chief Justice Earl Warren read the Court's ruling. He said, "We conclude that in the field of public education the doctrine of 'separate but equal' has no place."

The Supreme Court decision was momentous. It meant that school segregation would no longer be allowed. The black community celebrated. Marshall was thrilled. He later recalled, "I was so happy, I was numb."

Many people in the southern states were angry that the Court had meddled in state business. Many people resisted change in the schools. The integration of schools would face many barriers. Governors and lawmakers in the South were afraid to push for school changes. Most southern voters were white. Politicians did not want to take an unpopular stand and support school integration. As the beginning of the 1954 school year approached, the South prepared for change, protests, and violence.

Some schools did accept the *Brown v. Board of Education* decision right away. Baltimore, Maryland,

Thurgood Marshall went on to become the first black justice on the Supreme Court. He served on the Court from 1967 to 1991.

officials applied the ruling. In September of 1954, the city's 189 schools were opened to both black and white children. Angry whites protested outside a dozen schools, however. By October, tensions had risen, and fights broke out in the streets.

In northern Virginia, blacks attended previously all-white schools with few problems. Southern Virginia schools, however, put up a fight. The state's governor, Thomas Stanley, declared, "I shall use every legal means at my command to continue segregated schools in Virginia."

Governor Stanley was not the only high-ranking politician who felt this way. Governors in many southern states opposed the Court's new ruling. They refused to integrate public schools. North Carolina passed a law making local school boards responsible for integration. The law meant that parents would have to file individual lawsuits every time a school refused to integrate. This slowed down integration.

In 1955, the Supreme Court added to its first decision in *Brown*. The Court said that school integration should take place with "all deliberate speed." This decision, called *Brown II*, gave southern states a better chance to drag their feet. "All deliberate speed" did not name a specific deadline for integration. Slow-moving school boards claimed they were moving as fast as they could, even if they were moving slowly on purpose.

In Washington DC, Bryant Bowles founded the National Association for the Advancement of White People. He wanted to stop integration any way he could. Bowles wanted whites to stop their children from attending integrated schools.

Black students walking toward a newly integrated
school in Tennessee in December of 1954

President Dwight D. Eisenhower was uneasy about the Court's decision in *Brown II*. He knew integration would not be quick or easy. Eisenhower said, "The fellow who tries to tell me that you can do these things by force is just plain nuts." Eisenhower did not want to use his power as president to change southern opinions. However, the situation in Little Rock, Arkansas, forced him to take action.

President Eisenhower stated that schools must obey the Supreme Court's ruling and integrate.

Arkansas Governor Orval Faubus speaking out against school integration in 1959

Chapter Five

BROWN v. BOARD'S IMPACT

n 1957, the governor of Arkansas, Orval Faubus, tested the Supreme Court's decision. He ordered the state's **National Guard** to prevent nine black students from entering Little Rock Central High School. These students became known as the Little Rock Nine. They were pushed and prodded by white students while trying to enter the school. Violence soon broke out.

President Eisenhower ordered U.S. Army troops to Little Rock to keep the peace. Soldiers lined up on both sides of the nine black students and escorted them into the school. Little Rock Central High now had an integrated student body. At the end of the school year, Governor Faubus

The Arkansas National Guard had to escort black students into Little Rock Central High School on September 25, 1957.

closed all public schools in Little Rock for one year. The Supreme Court ruled that closing Little Rock's schools to avoid integration was unconstitutional. The schools reopened the following year.

The Little Rock event was one of many battles won for school integration. Each time a school district tried to prevent integration, supporters of *Brown v. Board of Education* stepped forward. The process was slow. Attempts to block integration arose at every level.

In 1961, a black student named James Meredith wanted to study at the University of Mississippi. As a Mississippi resident, Meredith had the right to attend the university. But the school remained all-white, even after the Court's decision in *Brown v. Board of Education*. After the school rejected Meredith's application, he sued the university.

Meredith lost his case in Mississippi but won on an appeal that was heard by the Supreme Court. When Meredith tried to sign up for classes, however, university officials refused to admit him. Finally, President John F. Kennedy ordered Mississippi's National Guard to protect Meredith so he could register at the school. After protests in which two people were killed, Meredith began classes and later graduated from the university.

Black students such as the Little Rock Nine and James Meredith led the way for other blacks. Slowly, more public schools and state universities accepted

One of the Little Rock Nine students graduated from Little Rock Central High in 1958. When Little Rock schools reopened in 1959, two more returned to Little Rock Central High for their senior year. They graduated in 1960.

A woman stopping black students from entering a Kentucky school in 1956

black students. The opportunities promised at the end of the Civil War were finally becoming a reality.

The *Brown v. Board of Education* decision was a milestone for black rights and equality. Many people consider it to be the event that led to the **civil rights movement**. It was certainly a major victory. But the ruling did not lead to as much change as some people had hoped.

It did not automatically end all segregation in the South. Black children who attended schools with white children were still banned from public parks. They still rode in the backs of buses and drank from "colored-only" water fountains.

By 1972, about 90 percent of southern schools had integrated. That did not mean all schools had a racial balance, however. Since black children went to schools near their homes, which were often in all-black neighborhoods, many schools still had mostly black students or mostly white students.

In the 1970s, schools used busing in an attempt to create more balance. White students were bused to mostly black schools, and black students were bused to mostly white schools. Although busing did improve integration, it was costly and did not work very well. No one wanted children to have to travel far when a good school was just a few blocks away. The practice of busing to integrate schools was eventually phased out. Children once again attended their neighborhood schools.

Thousands of blacks have graduated from high schools, colleges, and universities since 1954. They have used their educations to make valuable contributions in every field. Many of those contributions would not have happened without *Brown v. Board of Education*.

Because of the *Brown* ruling, spending in public schools is now based on the number of students, regardless of race. Students of all backgrounds take part in sports, the arts, and all other school activities together. *Brown v. Board of Education* may not have delivered immediate results, but this single lawsuit brought about monumental change for the country's children. All U.S. citizens have gained from the equal education that black parents and Thurgood Marshall and his legal team fought for decades ago.

Black and white girls standing in line in their classroom in 1955

TIME LINE

1863
Abraham Lincoln, the sixteenth U.S. president, issues the Emancipation Proclamation.

1868
The Fourteenth Amendment takes effect. It gives full constitutional rights to all black people.

1875
Congress passes the Civil Rights Act of 1875. This outlaws discrimination in hotels, theaters, and other public places.

1896
The U.S. Supreme Court decision in *Plessy v. Ferguson* allows states to provide separate but equal facilities for blacks and whites.

1909
The National Association for the Advancement of Colored People (NAACP) is formed to lead the fight for civil rights for blacks.

1938

The Supreme Court rules that states with graduate programs for whites have to offer "separate but equal" programs for blacks.

1947

Levi Pearson sues his local school board in South Carolina to get school buses for his children. He loses the case.

1950

The Supreme Court rules that the University of Oklahoma must end its segregation policies.

1952

The Supreme Court combines cases from Delaware, Kansas, South Carolina, Virginia, and Washington DC. It hears the case arguments under the heading of *Brown v. Board of Education*.

1954

The Supreme Court rules segregation in public schools to be unconstitutional in *Brown v. Board of Education*.

1955

In *Brown II*, the Supreme Court says that school integration should take place with "all deliberate speed."

1956

The Supreme Court outlaws segregation on public transportation.

1957

Escorted by U.S. Army troops, nine black students integrate Little Rock Central High School in Little Rock, Arkansas.

1962

James Meredith becomes the first black student at the University of Mississippi.

1964

President Lyndon Johnson signs the Civil Rights Act of 1964. Segregation in hotels, restaurants, stadiums, and other public places becomes illegal.

Glossary

aftermath
(*af*-tur-math)
Aftermath is the period of time following a harmful event. The aftermath of slavery included segregation and discrimination toward blacks.

amendment
(uh-*mend*-munt)
An amendment is a change made to a law or an official document. An amendment to the U.S. Constitution gave black people full constitutional rights.

appeal
(uh-*peel*)
An appeal is a legal procedure that allows for a court ruling to be reviewed in a higher court. The NAACP filed for an appeal for *Brown v. Board of Education*.

civil rights movement
(*siv*-il *rites moov*-munt)
The struggle for equal rights for blacks in the United States during the 1950s and 1960s is often called the civil rights movement. Many people believe the *Brown v. Board of Education* ruling led to the civil rights movement.

Constitution
(kon-stuh-*too*-shun)
The Constitution is the written document containing the principles by which the United States is governed. The Supreme Court rules on cases based on the U.S. Constitution.

constitutional
(kon-stuh-*too*-shun-ul)
Something that is constitutional relates to the U.S. Constitution. Blacks were often denied their constitutional rights.

discriminate
(diss-*krim*-ih-nayt)
When people discriminate, they treat others unfairly based on differences of race, gender, religion, or culture. Some whites discriminated against blacks based on the color of their skin.

docket
(*dok*-it)
A docket is a list of court cases to be heard. The *Brown v. Board* court case was on the Supreme Court's docket in 1951.

doctrine
(*dok*-trin)
A doctrine is a statement of government policy. The "separate but equal" doctrine stated that racial segregation was allowed.

graduate school
(*graj*-oo-it *skool*)
Graduate school is a level of school higher than college. The NAACP first fought for equal education at a graduate school.

integration
(in-tuh-*gray*-shun)
Integration is the act of allowing different race, class, or ethnic groups to be together in public facilities. After the *Brown v. Board* ruling, racial integration was mandatory in public schools.

lawsuit
(*law*-soot)
A lawsuit is a legal case brought against a person or a group. The NAACP filed a lawsuit to challenge school segregation.

minority groups
(mye-*nor*-uh-tee *groops*)
Minority groups are small groups of people that have often been discriminated against. The NAACP worked to gain civil rights for minority groups.

National Guard
(*nash*-uh-nul *gard*)
The National Guard is a volunteer military group that has units in each U.S. state. Governor Orval Faubus ordered the Arkansas National Guard to keep black students out of a white school.

plaintiffs
(*playn*-tifs)
Plaintiffs are the people who file lawsuits. The parents and students represented in *Brown v. Board of Education* were the plaintiffs in the case.

poverty
(*pov*-ur-tee)
Poverty is the state of being poor. Unequal education often led to low-paying jobs and poverty for blacks.

segregation
(seg-ruh-*gay*-shun)
Segregation is the act of keeping race, class, or ethnic groups apart. Before the *Brown v. Board* ruling, racial segregation was allowed in public schools.

FURTHER INFORMATION

Books

Haskins, James. *Separate, but Not Equal: The Dream and the Struggle*. New York: Scholastic, 2002.

Landau, Elaine. *The Civil Rights Movement in America*. Danbury, CT: Children's Press, 2007.

McNeese, Tim. *The Civil Rights Movement: Striving for Justice*. New York: Chelsea House, 2007.

McNeese, Tim. *Plessy v. Ferguson: Separate But Equal*. New York: Chelsea House, 2008.

Taylor-Butler, Christine. *Thurgood Marshall*. New York: Scholastic Library, 2006.

Walker, Paul Robert. *Remember Little Rock: The Time, the People, the Stories*. New York: National Geographic, 2009.

Videos

Black, White, and Brown. KTWU Productions, 2004.

The Road to Brown. California Newsreel, 1990.

With All Deliberate Speed. Anchor Bay, 2004.

Web Sites

Visit our Web page for links about *Brown v. Board of Education*:

http://www.childsworld.com/links

NOTE TO PARENTS, TEACHERS, AND LIBRARIANS: We routinely verify our Web links to make sure they are safe, active sites—so encourage your readers to check them out!

INDEX

Appeals, 6, 14–16, 25

Belton (Bulah) v. Gebhart, 14, 15
Belton, Ethel, 15
Bolling, Spottswood, Jr., 16
Bolling v. Sharpe, 14, 16
Briggs, Harry, 14
Briggs v. Elliot, 13, 14
Brown, Oliver, 16
Brown II, 20, 22
Brown v. Board of Education, 7, 16, 17–20, 25–27
Brown v. Board of Education of Topeka, 14, 16
Bulah, Sarah, 15
busing, 26–27

Civil rights movement, 26
Clark, Kenneth, 19
court cases. See names of individual cases

Davis v. County School Board of Prince Edward County, 13, 14

Eisenhower, Dwight D., 22, 23

Faubus, Orval, 23–24
Fourteenth Amendment, 8, 9, 17

Georgia, 12

Houston, Charles, 12

Integration, 6, 19–20, 22–23, 25–27

Jim Crow laws, 8–9
Johns, Barbara Rose, 14

Kansas, 14, 16
Kennedy, John F., 25

Little Rock, Arkansas, 23, 25
Little Rock Central High School, 23, 25
Little Rock Nine, 23, 25
Louisiana, 9

Marshall, Thurgood, 6, 12, 17–18, 19, 27
Maryland, 19–20
McLaurin, George, 5–6
Meredith, James, 25

National Association for the Advancement of Colored People (NAACP), 6, 7, 12, 13, 14, 15, 16, 17, 18
National Guard, 23, 25
North Carolina, 20

Parent involvement, 12, 13–16, 27
Pearson, Levi, 6
Plessy, Homer, 9
Plessy v. Ferguson, 6, 9, 10, 13, 17

School. See under segregation
segregation,
    public places, 8–10, 26
    school, 6, 7, 10, 12, 13–16, 18–20, 26
    "separate but equal" doctrine, 5, 6–7, 9–10, 13, 15, 16, 18, 19
slavery, 8
South, 8, 10, 19–20, 26
South Carolina, 6, 10, 13, 14
Stanley, Thomas, 20

University of Mississippi, 25
University of Oklahoma, 5–6
U.S. Civil War, 8, 26
U.S. Constitution, 8, 9, 25
U.S. District Court, 9, 16
U.S. Supreme Court, 5, 6, 7, 9, 16, 17–19, 20, 23, 25

Vinson, Fred, 17
Virginia, 13, 14, 20

Warren, Earl, 7, 17, 19
Washington DC, 14, 16, 20